I0797703

XTREME SNAKES

# ANACONDAS

BY S.L. HAMILTON

A&D Xtreme
An imprint of Abdo Publishing | abdopublishing.com

Printed in China.
032018
092018

Editor: John Hamilton
Copy Editor: Bridget O'Brien
Graphic Design: Sue Hamilton
Cover Design: Candice Keimig and Pakou Moua
Cover Photo: iStock
Interior Photos & Illustrations: Alamy-pgs 12-13 & 30-31; AP-pgs 24-25; Getty-pgs 15, 16-17 & 26-27; iStock-pgs 30 (inset) & 32; Lutz Dirksen-pgs 20-21; Minden Pictures-pgs 4-5, 14, 18-19, 22-23 & 28-29; Science Source-pgs 8-9 & 10-11; Shutterstock-pgs 1 & 2-3; Toni Kaarttinen-pgs 6-7.

Library of Congress Control Number: 2017963897
Publisher's Cataloging-in-Publication Data
Names: Hamilton, S.L., author.
Title: Anacondas / by S.L. Hamilton.
Description: Minneapolis, Minnesota : Abdo Publishing, 2019. | Series: Xtreme snakes | Includes online resources and index.
Identifiers: ISBN 9781532115998 (lib.bdg.) | ISBN 9781532156922 (ebook)
Subjects: LCSH: Anaconda--Juvenile literature. | Constrictors (Snakes)--Juvenile literature. | Snakes--Juvenile literature. | Reptiles--Juvenile literature. | Herpetology--Juvenile literature.
Classification: DDC 597.967--dc23

# Contents

# Anacondas

Anacondas are native to South America. These huge snakes are constrictors. They use their muscular bodies to squeeze their prey to death. They have rows of sharp teeth, but do not inject venom. Anacondas are sometimes called "water boas." They spend much of their time in the water. They are some of the largest and strongest, yet most shy and solitary, snakes on Earth.

***XTREME FACT –* *The longest verified anaconda was 30 feet (9 m) in length. That's nearly the same as 5 twin-size mattresses lined up end-to-end.***

Green Anaconda

# Body Parts

**Anacondas' scientific genus name, *Eunectes*, means "good swimmer."**

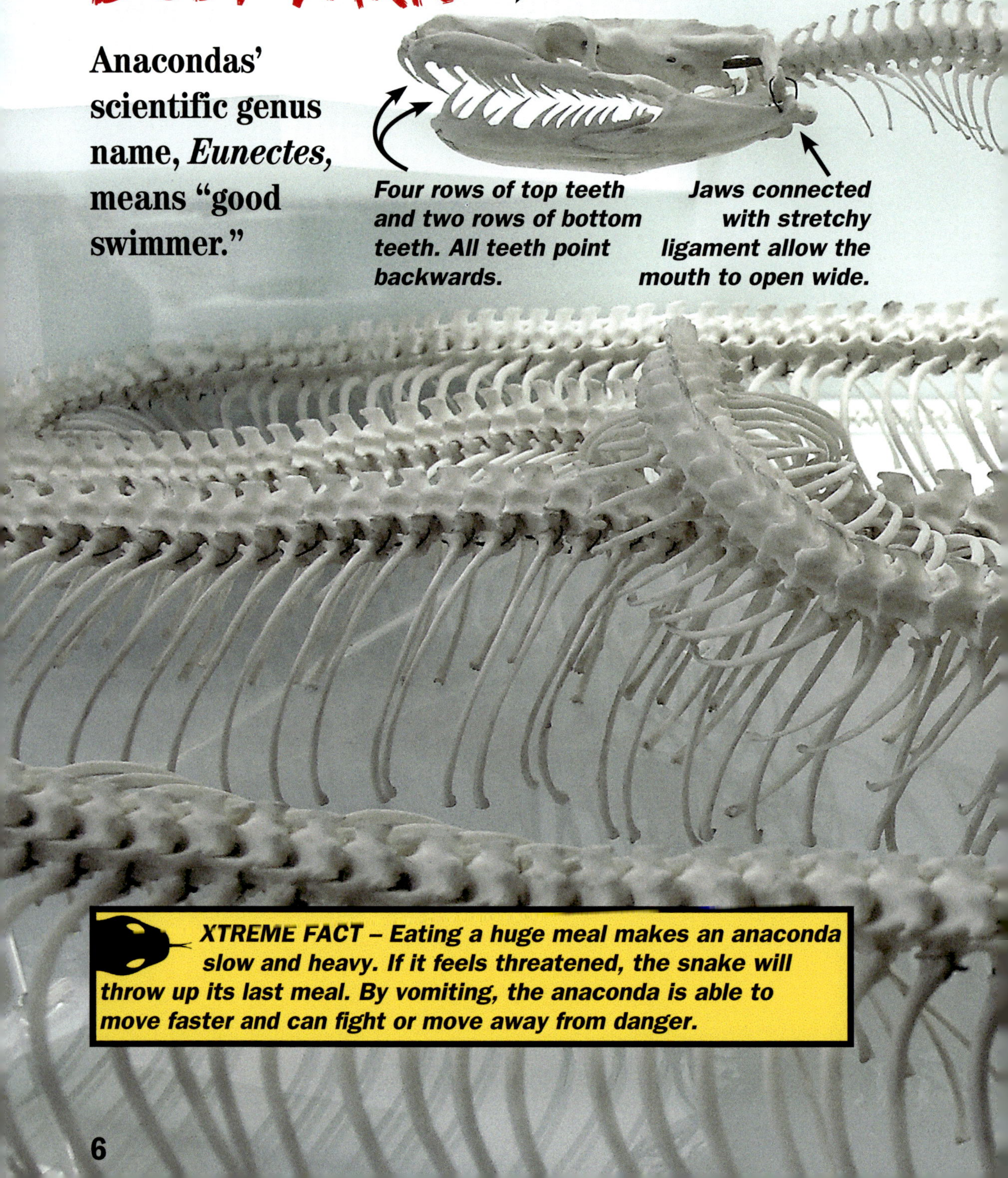

***XTREME FACT – Eating a huge meal makes an anaconda slow and heavy. If it feels threatened, the snake will throw up its last meal. By vomiting, the anaconda is able to move faster and can fight or move away from danger.***

Anacondas have eyes and nostrils on top of their heads. This allows them to keep their bodies mostly hidden underwater while swimming and hunting for prey.
Nostril
Ribs

# Hunting

Anacondas hunt using constriction. They eat their prey whole. They are ambush hunters, and often hunt at night. They lie in wait for prey to approach. When close enough, anacondas grab their victims and hold them in their strong, teeth-filled jaws.

Anacondas wind their bodies around their victims and squeeze. The prey dies from being crushed (internal bleeding) or because it can no longer breathe, either because the lungs can't expand or from drowning.

***XTREME FACT* – *Anacondas can hold their breath underwater for up to 10 minutes. The average person in good health may be able to hold their breath for about 2 minutes.***

# Prey

Anacondas only eat when they are hungry. They are not picky eaters, swallowing whole whatever prey they capture. They hunt fish, frogs, turtles, caimans, other snakes, and birds in the water. On the shoreline, they will also go after whatever comes near the water for a drink. This includes large prey such as capybaras, tapirs, deer, wild pigs, and even jaguars. Anacondas eat every few days or months, depending on how big a meal they last ate.

A green anaconda rests after eating a capybara. The bulge in the middle of the snake shows how its body expanded to make room for the large meal.

**XTREME FACT – Anacondas eat prey much bigger than themselves. They have large, stretchy ligaments that connect their top and bottom jaws. This allows them to open their mouths very wide to eat large victims.**

# HABITAT

There are four species of anacondas: green, yellow, Bolivian, and dark-spotted. All are native to South America. They make their homes in swamps, marshes, rain forests, and slow-moving rivers and streams. It is much easier for them to move their huge bodies through water.

***XTREME FACT – Green anacondas are apex predators. That means they are at the top of the food chain. Only humans attack a full-grown anaconda.***

*A green anaconda at its marshy home in Venezuela, South America.*

# NESTING

Up to a dozen anaconda males will mate with a female in a "breeding ball." Several males wrap themselves around the much larger female. Once pregnant, the female will produce many eggs.

A green anaconda breeding ball with one female and about 10 males.

***XTREME FACT – Anaconda females are cannibals. They may eat smaller male anacondas who have tried to mate with her. Since she will not eat for the 6-7 months while she is pregnant, the nearby male is a convenient meal for her.***

The eggs hatch inside the female's body. She gives birth to 20-80 live babies. This is called being "ovoviviparous." The babies are born in a clear sac in shallow water. They are 12 to 24 inches (30 to 61 cm) in length. They break out of the sac. The mother does not stay with them, but they can swim and hunt from birth. Baby anacondas eat small fish, mice, and lizards.

*A man holds a baby anaconda born in a zoo.*

# Green Anacondas

The green anaconda is both the largest anaconda and the heaviest snake in the world. The Asiatic reticulated python is the longest snake. But in weight, the female green anaconda wins.

*A green anaconda weighing about 220 pounds (100 kg) is held up by a team of adventurers in Guyana.*

The largest scientifically measured anaconda was 28 feet (8.5 m) long, with a girth (distance around the biggest part of its body) of 44 inches (112 cm). Researchers estimated her weight at a massive 500 pounds (227 kg). Green anacondas live about 10 years in the wild.

***XTREME FACT – Female anacondas are much larger than males. The average size of a female is 15 feet (4.5 m) and the average size of a male is 9 feet (2.7 m).***

# Yellow Anacondas

Yellow anacondas are also known as Parguayan anacondas. They are one of the smallest of their species, growing to an average of 10 feet (3 m) in length. That is about the length of one-and-a-half king-size beds! They weigh 55 to 77 pounds (25 to 35 kg).

Yellow anacondas are known as aggressive snakes, but they are still hunted for their beautiful skin. They live for 10-20 years in the wild.

***XTREME FACT – The yellow anaconda's skin is used to make purses, shoes, and belts. However, few people want to hunt this fierce snake.***

# Bolivian Anacondas

Bolivian anacondas, or Beni anacondas, are only found in the wild in Bolivia, South America. These snakes grow up to 14 feet (4.3 m) and live 10-12 years.

**XTREME FACT – Measuring an anaconda is extremely difficult. The snake does not typically stretch out long and straight. Sometimes people try to measure an anaconda's shed skin, but that is also likely stretched out longer than the actual snake.**

# Dark-Spotted Anacondas

Dark-spotted anacondas are also called DeSchauensee's anacondas. These snakes are native to Brazil, Guyana, and French Guiana. They look a lot like yellow anacondas, except the yellow on their body is slightly more greenish and their spots are bigger and wider. They average 9 feet (2.7 m) in length and live about 10 years in the wild.

***XTREME FACT – DeSchauensee's anacondas were named after birding specialist Rodolphe Meyer de Schauensee. He brought the snake back from a 1924 trip to South America and donated it to the Philadelphia Zoo.***

# Snake Handlers

Most people never want to meet an anaconda. But some people handle them in their work. A few zoos keep anacondas. They hire herpetologists who go to college to learn about reptiles and amphibians. These specialists are trained to safely handle these huge and dangerous snakes. Some people hunt anacondas for their skin. Others hunt the snakes to protect their livestock or families and pets. Some people choose anacondas as exotic pets. However, these snakes quickly become too big for people's homes. Anacondas also release a bad odor when they are bothered.

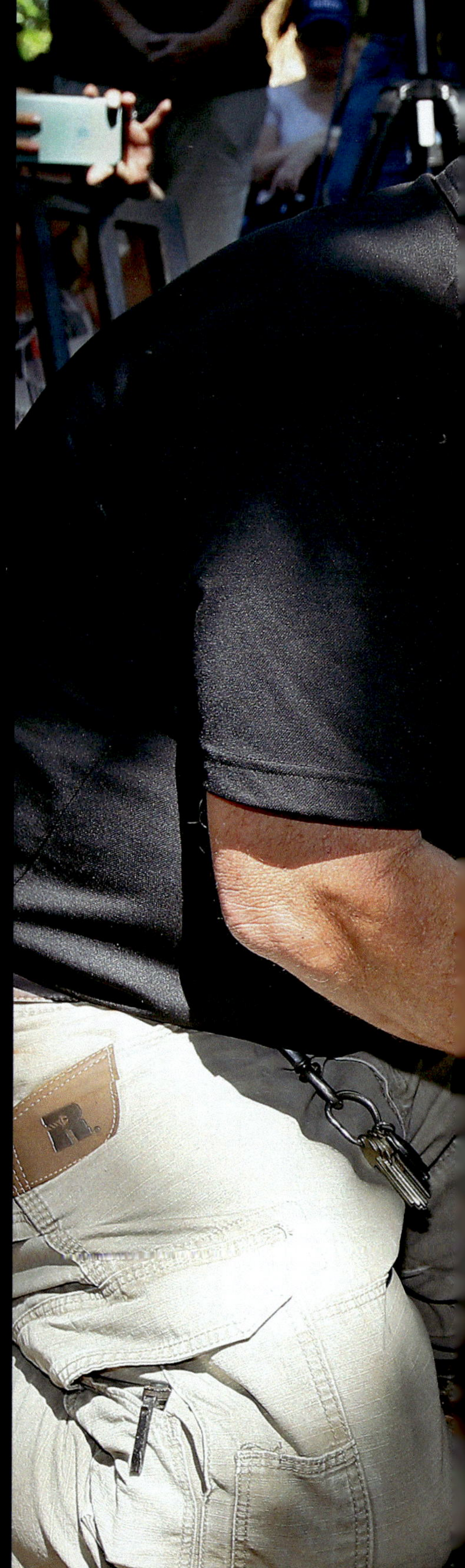

A herpetologist and a veterinarian examine an 18-year-old female green anaconda at the Oklahoma City Zoo.

# If You Are Attacked

Anacondas only attack a person if they are starving or threatened. However, if someone is in an anaconda's grip, try these defenses:

1) Call for help IMMEDIATELY. Most people who have survived have had the help of other people. If the anaconda bites, you'll begin to lose blood. If the muscular coils wrap around your body, your lungs and internal organs will be crushed within minutes. Get help fast.

*Herpetologist Ross Allen goes underwater to capture a 12-foot (3.7-m) anaconda.*

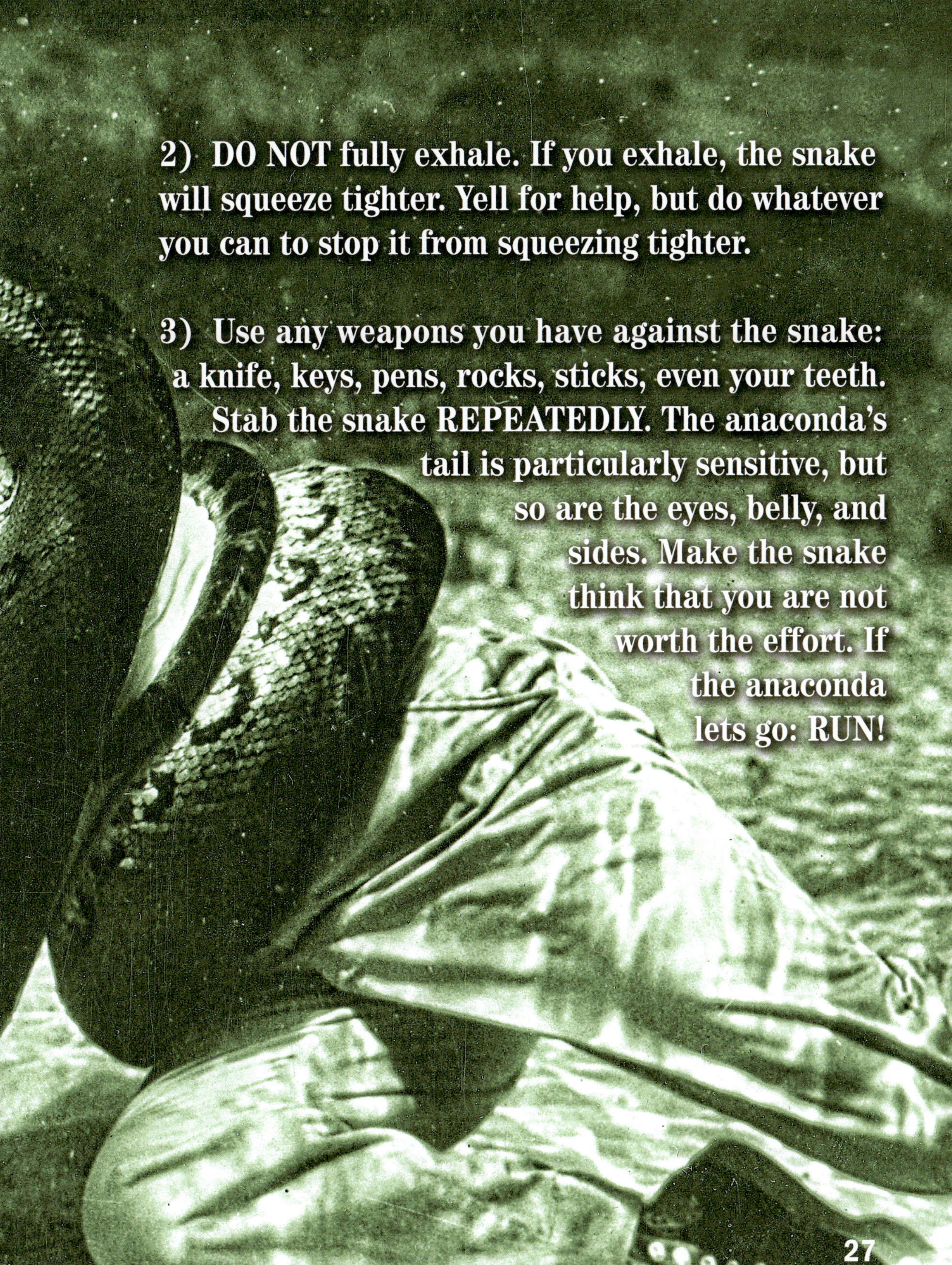

2) **DO NOT** fully exhale. If you exhale, the snake will squeeze tighter. Yell for help, but do whatever you can to stop it from squeezing tighter.

3) Use any weapons you have against the snake: a knife, keys, pens, rocks, sticks, even your teeth. Stab the snake **REPEATEDLY**. The anaconda's tail is particularly sensitive, but so are the eyes, belly, and sides. Make the snake think that you are not worth the effort. If the anaconda lets go: RUN!

# Are They Endangered?

Anacondas are not listed as endangered or threatened. They often live in South American areas where there are few people. Anacondas are not picky eaters, and eat whatever they can catch.

# Glossary

**Aggressive**
Likely to attack with, or without, a reason to do so.

**Ambush**
A surprise attack by something hiding nearby.

**Cannibal**
A creature that eats its own kind. Female anacondas are cannibals, sometimes eating smaller male anacondas.

**Capybara**
A very large rodent found in South America. Adults weigh about 108 pounds (49 kg). They live near water and are a frequent food for anacondas.

**Exotic Pets**
Unusual or rare pets that often come from another country. Sometimes exotic pets are illegal to own. Anacondas are considered an exotic pet.

**Food Chain**
The way living things get food, beginning with plants and moving up to small, medium, and large animals eating other animals.

**Genus**
A scientific category representing a group of living things that are all related to each other.

**Solitary**
Something that lives alone.

### Venom
A toxic liquid that some animals such as rattlesnakes, Gila monsters, and scorpions use for killing prey and for defense.

### Vomit
When an animal throws up or regurgitates the contents of its stomach.

# Online Resources

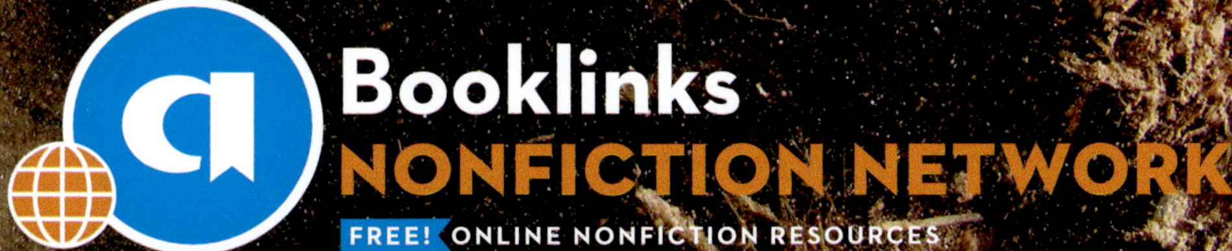


To learn more about anacondas, visit abdobooklinks.com. These links are routinely monitored and updated to provide the most current information available.

# INDEX